Victory Workbook I

A Bible study for victorious living

TERESA FAILOR

WESTBOW
PRESS
A DIVISION OF THOMAS NELSON

Reference Materials:
a. All Bible references are KJV unless otherwise noted
b. Young's Analytical Concordance to the Bible/Revised Edition
c. The American Heritage College Dictionary/Third Edition

WestBow Press books may be ordered through booksellers or by contacting:

WestBow Press
A Division of Thomas Nelson
1663 Liberty Drive
Bloomington, IN 47403
www.westbowpress.com
1-(866) 928-1240

ISBN: 978-1-4497-9145-2 (sc)
ISBN: 978-1-4497-9244-2 (e)

Library of Congress Control Number: 2013907308

Printed in the United States of America.

WestBow Press rev. date: 5/3/2013

Table of Contents

Preface

If you're anything like me, when you read a book, you start at Chapter 1 and skip the Preface. Please don't do that here. Check it out. If you don't (or haven't) internalize(ed) what is in the beginning, the rest of the information won't be as great a blessing for you.

"For God so loved the world, that he gave His only begotten Son that whosoever believeth in him *(Jesus)* should not perish, but have everlasting life." John 3: 16

"He that believeth on Him is not condemned: but he that believeth not is condemned already, because he hath not believed in the name of the only begotten Son of God *(Jesus)*." John 3: 18

"Neither is there salvation in any other: for there is none other name *(than Jesus—see context*) under heaven given among men, whereby we must be saved." Acts 4: 12

". . . Believe on the Lord Jesus Christ, and thou shalt be saved, . . ." Acts 16: 31

Romans 3: 23 states all have sinned and Romans 6: 23 tells us the wages of sin is eternal death and the gift of God is eternal life through believing in Jesus who paid the penalty on the cross at Calvary for your sins and mine. He rose from the dead on the third day and is now in Heaven with the Father. Also see Romans 8: 31-34 and Hebrews 7: 25.

In Romans 10: 9 & 10 you can learn how to partake of this gracious, wonderful gift of forgiveness and eternal life. Believe in your heart God has raised your savior Jesus from the dead and speak it with your mouth that you have received His gift (crucifixion/shedding of His sinless blood & resurrection) as payment for your sins. John 1:12 tells us "as many as received Him . . ."

Power for Living

God had provided the power to live for Him after receiving Jesus as Savior by receiving the Baptism in the Holy Spirit. See Acts 1: 8; 2: 4; Matthew 3: 11; Luke 11: 13 as well as others. (believe, ask, receive)

The body of Christ is an organism with many parts (I Cor. 12: 13-28; Eph. 4: 16; Col. 1: 18). By the same kind of definition, the Word of God is an organism. Hebrews 4: 12 states "The Word of God is living and active!" *Please see the rest of that scripture and the following verse.* I want to focus on part A.

There are so many wonderful teachings and teachers available to us (watch there will be some that are not so wonderful according to II Timothy 4: 3 and other scriptures) but they are not all anointed to teach the whole council of God. Remember, **no one** knows everything but God. Therefore, some discredit those they don't understand or don't agree with. Would it be better to refrain the tongue from speaking evil and—take what you need? Put the rest on a shelf; some day you might use it. Get into the Word and see what God says on each subject.

In this presentation, I am attempting to help bring various topics (it's impossible to address all the issues of life in one book) together for daily victorious living. We experience blessings, trials, sickness/healing, relationships, finances/giving, on and on and on.

Let's try to find a common denominator that allows the Word of God to work in all areas and decide what to focus on for total victory. Jesus is coming back and we don't know when! Let's not only be ready, let's enjoy the journey between now and then.

The only way these studies can be made "yours" is for you to get your revelation from God. Therefore; *I have placed blanks (   ) where there is a quote/word from the Bible in order for you to search the scriptures and find it for yourself.* Write the scripture reference in these blanks. The first one is done for you. There are answers at the end of each Topic; don't be surprised if you find others that apply because numerous scriptures could fill each blank.

Topic # 1

End Time Battle is in the Mind

1. Victorious Christians study the Word (*II Tim.2:15*), memorize the Word, meditate on the Word, believe the Word (*Jn. 17:17*), and act/speak the Word (Mk. 11:23-24). Worrying and caring more about what others think than what you care about the Word (*Phil. 4:5 & Mt. 6:24-34*) are enemies of Christ and of your victorious living.

2. Other things/interests need to be put aside and time made for the above! Abide in Him; that your joy might be full (&   ).

3. We need to live like we believe God. God and His Word are one (   ). If He said it, then it's true and a reality (&   ) for our lives. Thy Word is truth.

4. Let's look at what the Word of God says about the un-renewed mind. Mankind can have an unbelieving, defiled mind (   ) . . . . alienated and enemies in your mind by wicked works . . . (   ) Take a look at the end of that verse.

5. The children of wrath might fulfill the desires of the mind
(   ). Who are these children of wrath and do they
have to stay in that condition (   )?

6. Now let's see what we can find about the mind of our Savior
Jesus. Oh! The Word of God tells us to have the same
obedient servant mind that was in Christ Jesus (   ).
And we are not to faint in our mind (   ). What does
that mean? Ok, faint there means to relax, lack conviction or
courage *(b, c)*. Sounds like a big assignment but if we consider
what Jesus did, nothing should cause us to faint in our mind.

7. Can Satan really put thoughts into our mind? It looks like
the Word says so in (&   ) where the god
of this world hath blinded the minds. If it weren't so, why
would the Word of God tell us to gird up the loins of our mind
(   ); the NIV translation is to prepare your mind and
be self-controlled. So, what does that tell you about your job? (I
don't mean about your place of employment!) Guard your mind;
fill it with God's thoughts, cast down imaginations and every
high thing that exalteth itself against the knowledge of God
(   ).

8. The mind can only be renewed with the Word of God
(   ). Casting down imaginations and every high
thing that exalts itself against the knowledge of God. Bring
into captivity every thought to the obedience of Christ

(   ). Believe God's Word, not what you can see, feel, or touch. Get your thoughts, and believing correct and everything else will fall into place according to God's Word (&   &   ).

9. In (   ) we read we are not to walk in the vanity (uselessness *(b)*) of the mind. Then, we see a reprobate mind in (   ) and the mind serving God but the flesh serving sin (   ). There's hope; look at (   ).

10. Here we go—I found it! It mentions a pure mind in (   ). Their pure minds were stirred up being made mindful of the words of the Prophets, Apostles and the Lord Jesus Christ.

11. God has not given us a spirit of fear but of (   ) power, love, and a sound mind.

12. Let's look at why God has been so gracious and giving toward us. This will help us focus/think on God and the things of God. The very first scripture we usually learn regarding salvation is God so **loved** that he **gave** (   ). Jesus loves us like Father God loves Him; (   ) "As the Father has loved me . . .". That's awesome and the Father (&   ) also loves us. Something else to think about—we are overcomers. The Word says "Who is he that

3

overcomes the world . . . (   ). It's all been done for
us by Jesus. He redeemed us because he loves us!

13. After the mind has been made new in Christ, we are to be of
the same mind with no divisions among us (   ).

14. Arm yourselves likewise with the same mind (   ) as
Christ; having compassion on one another (   ).

15. This will bring us into unity (   ) with one mind
striving together for the faith of the gospel; esteeming others
better than self (   ).

16. Make every effort to keep the unity of the Spirit
(NIV   ). Do you remember what God said at the
Tower of Babel when the people were in unity? It says nothing
will be restrained from them which they have imagined to do?
Better take a look. I'll give you that one—Gen. 11: 6. He really
did say that. Unity is powerful! Can we even imagine how our
wonderful Father God longs for his "kids" to be in unity. In the
New Testament (   ) we read about becoming mature
and in the unity of the faith. We are to not only love God but
love one another (   ).

17. Now what are we supposed to do toward God with
those minds? We are to love Him with all our mind
(&   ) and (   ) "Thou wilt

keep him in perfect peace, whose mind is stayed on thee (don't stop now that's not the end) because he trusteth on thee. Trust ye in the Lord forever; for in the Lord JEHOVAH is everlasting strength".

18. We are to fill our minds with God's Word. Studying the Word will develop our faith (   ). Faith comes by hearing the Word.

II Cor. 10:4-5 instructs us to cast down every imagination that exalts itself against the knowledge of God and bring into captivity every thought to the obedience of Christ. Controlling our mind with the Word of God is absolutely necessary in order to "let no corrupt communication proceed out of our mouth" (Eph. 4: 29). To get the mouth obedient to Christ, we must first take a look at what our mind turns those thoughts into—imaginations that form our attitudes.

Topic #1   **Answer Sheet, End Time Battle is in the Mind**

1. (II Tim. 2:15); (Jn. 17:17); (Mk. 11:23-24); (Phil. 4:5 & Mt. 6: 24-34)

2. (Jn. 15: 11-12, 16: 24 & Rom. 15:13)

3. (Jn. 1: 1); (Jn. 17: 17 & 8: 32)

4. (Titus 1:15); (Col. 1:21)

5. (Eph. 2: 3); (Eph. 2: 4-9)

6. (Phil. 2: 5); (Heb. 12: 3)

7. (II Cor. 4: 4 & Eph. 6:12); (I Pet. 1: 13); (II Cor. 10:5)

8. (Eph. 4: 23); (II Cor. 10: 4-5); (II Cor. 10: 7 & Heb. 11:1 & Jn. 7: 24)

9. (Eph. 4:17); (Rom. 1:28); (Rom. 7: 25); (Rom. 8: 1)

10. (II Pet. 3: 1)

11. (II Tim. 1: 7)

12. (Jn. 3:16); (Jn. 15:9); (Jn. 16:27 & Mt. 7: 9-11); (I Jn. 5: 4-5)

13. (I Cor. 1: 10)

14. (I Pet. 4:1); (I Pet. 3:8)

15. (Phil. 1: 27); (Phil. 2:3)

16. (Eph. 4:3); (Eph. 4:13); (I Jn. 4: 10-11)

17. (Mt. 22: 37 & Mk. 12: 30); (Isa. 26: 3)

18. (Rom. 10:17)

End of Topic # 1

Notes:

Topic # 2

Attitude/Forgiveness

We will begin by examining what attitudes are and where they come from. We are a spirit that has a soul and lives in a body (I Thess. 5:23). The spirit is the part of us the Holy Spirit indwells when we receive Jesus as Lord and Saviour. We can see what the body is. The soul (Col. 3:1) is our feelings (emotions), thinking, and willingness (will) to believe and behave in a particular manner.

The soul receives its impressions from the outer world. These impressions are gathered by the senses (sight, hearing, taste, smell, and touch). The soul examines these impressions through the intellect, reason, memory, imagination, and our experiences.

1. Attitudes are that state of mind that was decided on in our soul such as a feeling or disposition—which is a mood. Our soul uses our body to carry out what we have decided to do. Those activities could be sinful evil desires (& &),

2. or if we are consciously submitted to God and His Holy Word, they could be what the will (& &) of the Lord is. The fruit of the Spirit is listed in ( ).

3. God sees it all (   ).

The following are examples of negative/ hurtful attitudes with some scriptural responses:

4. <u>Anxiety</u> is the opposite of trusting God. Be anxious for nothing
   (   ). In Christ we have peace (&   ).
   Let the peace of God rule your heart (   ). We're
   going to study trust in another section.

5. <u>Depression</u> is feeling sad, despondent, gloomy, dejected,
   pressed down, or weak. This is the opposite of joyfulness
   so let's find out how to get joy. There is a sacrifice of joy
   (   ) and joy of forgiveness when King David said
   ". . . restore unto me the joy of thy salvation" (   ).
   The fullness of joy is found in the Gospel of John
   (&   ). The attitude of depression goes
   along with the next one, feeling unworthy. Meditating of what
   Jesus has done for us will bring joy.

6. If you have not received Jesus as Lord and Saviour, you are
   <u>unworthy</u>. Take a look at (&
   &   ) as to our worthiness in Christ Jesus.

7. Do you feel <u>untalented?</u> What does (   ) say about
   your abilities to do all things through Christ?

8. For someone who is feeling <u>lonely</u>, it's important to show yourself friendly to others (&   ).
   (   ) tells us we can be a friend of God.

9. A good word from God for someone who feels <u>unloved</u> would be that nothing can separate you from the love of God in Christ Jesus (   ).

10. <u>Anger</u> is caused by wounded feelings and could be varying degrees of displeasure such as resentment or indignation. We are to make a conscious decision to put off (get rid of) anger (&   ) along with other negative attitudes. We can make a decision to never be offended and love our enemies (   ).

11. We are to do all things without (   ) murmuring and complaining. That tells us what we are to do about a <u>critical</u> attitude.

God's Word can give us insight into all our attitudes. Attitudes relating to <u>hate, revenge, abuse, and unforgiveness</u> are addressed in the following scriptures:

12. Love your enemies, be merciful, (&   )
    and forgive (&   &   ). When you
    pray, forgive (   ).

13. Keep forgiving (&   ). Seventy times seven is referring to infinity.

14. If you forgive not (   ), you can not be forgiven. Unforgiveness can also cause illness and block healing in our body.

15. This scripture (   ) tells us what our heavenly Father will do if ye from your hearts forgive not everyone his brother their trespasses.

God has a lot to say about these destructive attitudes. Take a look at more of His solution:

16. We are to be swift to hear, slow to speak, and slow to anger (   ).

17. In Proverbs (   ) we can learn that the ability to decide responsibly will defer anger. The dictionary meaning of defer is to submit to the wishes of another through respect.

18. Bless them which persecute you, forgive because vengeance is mine says the Lord (&   ).

19. It appears that forgiveness is the key to getting attitudes straight with God. We are to be of one mind, have compassion, love one another, and be courteous (   ).

20. As a person thinks in his heart, so he is (   ). It is
    wise to keep the heart with all diligence; (   ) for out
    of it are the issues of life.

21. If you are still not convinced it's of the utmost importance to
    forgive everyone who has ever offended you, go back and look
    at what we learned about the consequences if you forgive not
    (&   ).

22. In addition to forgiveness from God, mercy will give us favor
    with God and man (   ).

23. I am crucified with Christ (   ) and He lives in me.
    That new person is renewed after the image of the creator
    (   ).

At this point, it is suggested that everyone working through this study
would talk to Father God and ask that the Holy Spirit reveal anyone
that you might need to forgive. Simply ask, wait a few seconds (that's
all it takes) and verbally forgive everyone who comes to mind. Then,
ask Jesus to forgive you for holding unforgiveness against that/those
person(s). Pray in Jesus name, amen.

Now we should be ready to see what the Bible says about our tongue.

Topic #2   Answer Sheet, Attitude/Forgiveness

1. (Col. 3: 5-9 & Eph. 4: 25-32 & Gal. 5:19-21)

2. (Eph. 5: 17-21 & Col. 3: 12-17 & Gal. 5: 16); (Gal. 5:22-26)

3. (Heb. 4: 13)

4. ((Phil. 4: 6); (Jn. 16: 33 & Isa. 26: 3); (Col. 3:15)

5. (Psa. 27: 6); (Psa. 51: 12); (Jn. 15:11 & 16: 23-24)

6. (II Cor. 5: 21 & Eph. 1: 7 & Psa. 121:1-9)

7. (Phil. 4: 13)

8. ((Prov. 3: 12 & Psa. 37: 4); (Jn. 15: 14)

9. (Rom. 8: 38-39)

10. (Eph. 4: 31 & Col. 3: 8); (Mt. 5: 44)

11. (Phil. 2: 14)

12. (Mt. 5: 44 & Lk. 6: 35-37); (Mt. 6:12 & Lk.11: 4 & Eph. 4:32); (Mk.11: 25)

13. (Mt. 18: 22 & Col. 3: 13)

14. (Mt. 6: 15)

15. (Mt. 18: 34-35)

16. (Jas. 1: 19)

17. (Prov. 19: 11)

18. (Rom. 12: 14-21 & Prov. 25: 21)

19. (I Pet. 3: 8-12)

20. (Prov. 23: 7); Prov. 4: 23)

21. (Mt. 6: 15 & Jas. 2: 13)

22. (Prov. 3: 3-4)

23. (Gal. 2: 20); (Col. 3: 10)

end of Topic # 2

Notes:

Topic # 3

Mouth/Speaking

Let's start with evil communication.

1. (   ) Every idle (unprofitable *(b)*) word . . . they will give account thereof." We will be held accountable for every word that comes out of our mouth."

2. Life and death are in the power of the tongue (   ).

3. In (   ) we see corrupt communication. God wouldn't mention corrupt communication if it was not an issue.

4. Let's look at some corrupt communication. In (   ) we can read that we are not to be a talebearer. A talebearer (   ) reveals secrets; therefore, meddle not with him that flattereth with his lips.

5. We learn in (   ) an evil man out of the evil treasure of his heart brings forth evil. And the devil (   ) is called the accuser of the brethren.

6. That evil heart sows strife, digs up evil and those lips (   ) are as a burning fire!

7. In (   ) we see that idleness leads to evil speaking.

8. Also, God's Word says that all liars will end up in
   (   ) the lake of fire. These speakings are all
   initiated in the mind. One must think the thought before it is
   spoken.

9. Murmuring and complaining (   ) were addressed under
   critical attitudes.

There is also good speaking that is pleasing to God:

10. Speak only those things that we are allowed to think on
    (   ) and according to that scripture it must be a
    good report.

11. Praise ye the Lord, O ye servants of the Lord, (   )
    praise the name of the Lord. Yes, that one says servants.

12. Thanks be to God which giveth us the victory (   )
    through our Lord Jesus Christ. And this one is talking to those
    who have the victory.

Do all the servants have the victory? Maybe not. Mankind can
speak both good and evil!

13. We can speak from the good treasure (   ) of the heart or speak evil.

14. (   ) Words can be both like piercing of a sword or they can be health.

15. Guarding the words of the mouth guards the soul (NIV   ); otherwise he shall have destruction (KJV   ).

16. We can speak good and evil out of the same mouth (   ).

17. If we have whatever we say, (   ) how do we fix this mouth?

How can we change our way of speaking?

18. Try this (   ). Offend not in word.

19. If that's too tough, try (   ) to put away a disobedient mouth.

20. (   ) Prayer . . . keep the door of my lips.

21. In (   ) we are instructed to bridle our tongue.

22. However, we read in (   ) that no man can tame the tongue. We need the power of the Holy Spirit and the Word of God for this one.

23. Study to show thyself approved unto God, (   ) rightly dividing the word of truth.

24. We can have the victory. Remember Romans 8: 1? Believe there is no condemnation to those in Christ Jesus (Do you fully understand what "in Christ Jesus" means? Did you read/do the Preface?) Walk after spiritual things not what pleases the flesh. Obey God. To receive salvation, we confessed with our mouth what we believed in our hearts (   ). That is the beginning.

25. No one knows what light has been revealed to others. Judge not, that you be not judged (   ).

We're only required to walk in the light/understanding of God's will/ Word that has been revealed to us individually. Check out what you hear by searching the Word of God. Jesus and His Word are one.

We feed our natural body several times a day. Should this be our guide for our spirit man? Think on this: If you don't feed your natural body it will die. What will happen if you never feed your spirit with the Word of God?

Look at the positive side of life. Celebrate each new day. Happiness is a choice; be happy on purpose! Minister grace to the hearers of your words, Gal. 4:29.

Additional study recommended is Proverbs 3: 1-18 & Proverbs 4: 20-27.

Let's now search the scriptures regarding ministering to Almighty God.

Topic # 3   **Answer Sheet, Mouth/Speaking**

1. (Mt. 12: 36)

2. (Prov. 18: 21)

3. (Eph. 4: 29-30)

4. (Lev. 19: 16); (Prov. 20: 19)

5. (Lk. 6: 45); (Rev. 12: 10)

6. (Prov. 16: 27-28)

7. (I Tim. 5: 13)

8. (Rev. 21: 8)

9. (Phil. 2: 14)

10. (Phil. 4: 8)

11. (Psa. 113: 1)

12. (I Cor. 15: 57)

13. (Lk. 6: 45)

14. (Prov. 12: 18)

15. (Prov. 13: 3 NIV & KJV)

16. (Jas. 3: 10)22. (Jas. 3: 8)

17. (Mk. 11: 22-23)

18. (Jas. 3: 2)

19. (Prov. 4: 20-23)

20. (Psa. 141: 3)

21. (Jas. 1: 26)

22. (Jas. 3: 8)

23. (II Tim. 2: 15)

24. (Rom. 10: 8)

25. (Mt. 7: 1-2)

End of Topic # 3

Notes:

Topic # 4

Praise/Worship—Section # 1

Section # 1 covers praise that leads to worship.

Praise:

What is praise? The American Heritage College dictionary states 1. an expression of approval, commendations, or admiration 2. The extolling or exaltation of a deity, ruler or, hero. That sounds like what we're looking for to begin worship of God.

Following are some meanings of original praise words in the Bible:

1. todah—sacrifice of praise and thanksgiving (
   &   ). Who so offers praise glorifies God.

2. barak—declare blessed and kneel. This is what we find in
   (   )

3. yadah—to stretch out the hand. (&   )

Now we will continue with who, how, what, when, where and why.

4. Who are we to praise & worship? Let's look at (   )
   to see it's the name of the Lord. Praise ye the Lord.

5. In (   ) we find more directions to praise and worship; the Lord he is God; it is he that has made us. But who is to praise Him?

6. We find men praising Him, (   );

7. poor and needy praise His Name (   ).

8. All people praise in (&   ); and

9. all nations should praise Him (   ).

10. <u>How and with what</u> are we to praise the Lord? Start with greatly and with our whole heart (&   ).

11. Then we can sing (   ) and dance (   ).

12. Dance like King David danced (   ) and like Miriam the Prophetess, the sister of Aaron, and all the women danced playing the timbrel, an ancient instrument similar to a tambourine (c), and singing (   ).

13. Try lifting the hands (   );

14. clapping and shouting (   ).

15. More of "with what" are we to praise is the harp (   );
    psaltery, an ancient stringed instrument (c) (   ); and
    again

16. in song (   ).

17. When should we praise the Lord? The Psalms give us excellent
    directions regarding praise. As an answer to when, we read
    "while I live" (   );

18. "when we enter His gates" (   );

19. "forever" (&   &   );

20. and at all times (   ). You can find more scriptures
    but not more time than all times and forever.

21. Where are we to praise the Lord?

    Answers to that are: among the people (   );

22. in the midst of the church (   );

23. in the assembly of the elders (   ); and

24. in the congregation (&   &   ). The
    above "at all times" would indicate alone as well as with people.

So <u>why</u> should we do all this? Here again, there are hundreds of reasons to praise God. We'll just look at some of them:

25. Let's start with our creation. We are fearfully and (   ) wonderfully made;

26. because He has heard and answered me and (   ) He is <u>my</u> God.

27. Thank and praise Him for His glorious name (   ).

28. If that's not enough, we can praise Him for
    (&   ) his mighty acts;

29. setting ambushes against the enemy (   );

30. for his mercy (&   &   )

31. or just because it's a good thing (   ).

32. What has Jesus provided for us? Believe on the Lord Jesus Christ and you will be saved! That's a pretty good reason without the others. He said I and the Father are one and He sent the Holy Spirit to us. Whosoever will receive Him (   )! I'll help you with this one. It's on page # 3.

33. In the New Covenant we find (   ) that we are a royal priesthood, a holy nation, God's own possession called out of darkness into His marvelous light.

Following is a Biblical example of praise and worship of Almighty God:

II Chronicles 5: 12-14 KJV:

"Also the Levites *which were* the singers, all of them of Asaph, of Heman, of Jeduthun, with their sons and their brethren, *being* arrayed in white linen, having cymbals and psalteries and harps, stood at the east end of the altar, and with them an hundred and twenty priests sounding with trumpets: It came even to pass, as the trumpeters and singers *were* as one, to make one sound to be heard in praising and thanking the Lord; and when they lifted up *their* voice with the trumpets and cymbals and instruments of musick, and praised the Lord, *saying*, For *he* is good; for his mercy *endureth* for ever: that *then* the house was filled with a cloud, *even* the house of the Lord; So that the priests could not stand to minister by reason of the cloud: for the glory of the Lord had filled the house of God."

What we have just studied regarding praise is pretty much summed up in Psalm 150 which is a suggested scripture to memorize:

<u>Who; where</u>—**Praise ye the Lord. Praise God in his sanctuary: praise him in the firmament of his power.**

<u>Why</u>—**Praise him for his mighty acts; praise him according to his excellent greatness.**

How—**Praise him with sound of the trumpet: praise him with the psaltery and harp.**

What—**Praise him with the timbrel and dance: praise him with stringed instruments and organs. Praise him upon the loud cymbals: praise him upon the high sounding cymbals.**

Who—**Let everything that hath breath praise the Lord. praise ye the Lord.**

Topic # 4   **Answer Sheet, Praise**

1. (Heb. 13: 15 & Psa. 50: 23)

2. (Psa. 72: 15)

3. (Isa. 12: 4 & Isa. 25: 1 & Psa. 54:6)

4. (Psa. 135: 1)

5. (Psa. 100: 3-4)

6. (Psa. 107: 8, 15, 21, 31)

7. (Psa. 74: 21)

8. (Psa. 67: 3, 5 & Psa. 45: 17)

9. (Psa. 117: 1)

10. (Psa. 109: 30 & 138: 1)

11. (Psa. 33: 2 & 28: 7); (Psa. 149: 3 & 150: 4)

12. (II Sam. 6:14); (Ex. 15: 20-21)

13. (I Tim. 2: 8)

14. (Psa. 47:1)

15. (Psa. 33: 2); (Psa. 71: 22)

16. (Psa. 28: 7 & Jere. 20:13)

17. (Psa. 46: 2)

18. (Psa. 100: 4)

19. (Psa. 52: 9 & 104: 33 & 145: 1)

20. (Psa. 34: 1)

21. (Psa. 108: 3)

22. (Heb. 2:12)

23. (Psa. 107:32)

24. (Psa. 38: 18 & 111: 1 & 107: 32)

25. (Psa. 139: 14)

26. (Psa. 118: 21, 28)

27. (I Chr. 29: 13)

28. (Psa. 28: 6 & 150: 20)

29. (II Chr. 20: 22)

30. (Psa. 20:21 & 106: 1 & 136: 2)

31. (Psa. 92: 1)

32. (Jn. 1:12); (Jn. 3: 16)

33. (I Pet. 2: 9)

end of Topic # 4

Notes:

The following section goes beyond the mouth and physical to "Worship in spirit and truth" (*See Power for Living at the beginning*).

Topic # 5

Praise/Worship—Section # 2

Worship in spirit and truth

Worship:

1. Praise is to lead us into <u>Worship</u> (&   ).
    The Creator God is the Lord, the Holy One, the First and
    (&   &   ) the Last. Following is a list of
    just some of God's names to see what they mean and observe
    more reasons why we should worship Him (b.):

    a. JEHOVAH-RAPHA, "the Lord that healeth" (   ).

    b. JEHOVAH-NISSI, "the Lord our banner" (   ).

    c. JEHOVAH-SHALOM, "The Lord our peace" (   ).

    d. JEHOVAH RA'AH, "The Lord my shepherd" (   ).

    e. JEHOVAH-TSIDKENU, "the Lord our righteousness"
        (   ).

    f. JEHOVAH-JIREH, "the Lord who provides" (   ).

g. JEHOVAH-SHAMMAH, "the Lord is there". (   ).

h. EL-ELYON, "the most high God". (   ).

i. EL-SHADDAI, "the God Almighty". (   ).

j. Adonai means Lord or Master. (&   ).

k. God is eternal (&   &   &   &   );

l. Omnipresent (&   &   &
    &   );

m. and He is Omniscient (&   &   &   ).

2. Oh! Isn't a lot of that teaching Old Covenant? Right. The once and for ever sacrifice has been offered. We're under a new dispensation; Jesus paid the price for sin, rose from the dead, and ascended to the Father; the Holy Spirit has come (   ); and now as we enter into his courts with praise we move into worship in spirit and in truth (   ).

3. First, let's check something out in the New Covenant. The Gospel of John was ". . . written that ye might believe that Jesus is the Christ, the Son of God; and that believing ye might have life through his name" (   ).

4. Think about the following list of names ascribed to Jesus in the Gospel of John as you fill in the blanks with <u>chapter numbers</u> starting with chapter 1:

a. The Word, God, Creator, Light, Lamb of God, Son of God, Rabbi, Messiah, He of whom Moses wrote (   );

b. Teacher come from God, Son of man, only begotten Son of God, Son of God, Light, Christ, Bridegroom, Above all, He whom God has sent (   );

c. The Lord, a Jew, a Prophet, Saviour of the world (   );

d. He that God the Father sealed, Bread of God, Bread of life, Living Bread, That Christ, Son of the living God (   );

e. Master, Lord, Light of the world, He who came from God, I Am (   );

f. Light of the world, Prophet, Son of God, Lord (   );

g. Good Shepherd, Door of the sheep, One with the Father (   );

h. Master, Life, the Christ, the Son of God, Lord (   );

i. King of Israel, King, Son of man, Light (   );

j. The Way, the Truth, the Life, in the Father & Father in Me, the Son (   );

k. True Vine (   );

l. King of the Jews, The Man, Son of God (   );

m. Jesus of Nazareth the King of the Jews (   ). And then in (   ) we read Jesus' directions that applies to us today as well, don't look at others, just follow Jesus.

5. Those who worship God in the spirit under the New Covenant put no confidence in the flesh (   ).

6. True believers are a spiritual house, a holy priesthood, to offer up spiritual sacrifices acceptable to God through Jesus Christ (   ). <u>As we meditate on who God is and what Jesus has done for us</u>, the Holy Spirit will move us into the realm of worshiping in Spirit and Truth. You may want to go back and review "Power for Living" at the beginning of the lessons.

7. All will one day worship God (   ).

Let's reflect for a moment. To get to the place just mentioned, we need to think right thoughts, speak right (God's) words, believe God's Word and act on God's Word. Does it require faith on our part to believe God is receiving our spiritual worship? Without faith it's impossible to please God (Heb. 11:6). Does the Holy Ghost power just automatically make it all work? Nothing is automatic—it's all a decision.

That thought in my mind could be my own or it could have been put in there by words, experiences or the enemy. That's where my attitudes come from. I speak that thought. As I think and speak, "that" thought gets down into my heart. No, not my blood pump—my spirit.

There's more to victory than what we've covered thus far. As a man thinks in his heart, the Bible says, so he is. The unsaved person is lost; the carnal person is in trouble; the born again person has access to the answer (*Power for Living scriptures at the beginning*) but you guessed it—it really is a choice and it's work! Oh! oh! I can see it now. I need faith to get it right. The next topic is hope/faith.

Topic # 5   Answer Sheet, Worship

1. (Psa. 95: 6-7, 96: 9); (Isa. 43: 15 & 44: 6 & Deut. 4:39)

    a. (Ex. 15: 26)
    b. (Ex. 17: 8-15)
    c. (Judg. 6: 24)
    d. (Psa. 23: 1)
    e. (Jere. 23: 6)
    f. (Gen. 22: 14)
    g. (Ezek. 48: 35)
    h. (Gen. 14: 18-20)
    i. (Ex. 6: 3)
    j. (Ex. 23: 17 & Isa. 10: 16, 33)
    k. (Ex. 15: 18 & Deut. 33: 27 & Neh. 9: 5 & Rev. 4: 8-10 & Psa. 90: 2)
    l. (Gen. 28: 15-16 & Deut. 4: 39 & Josh. 2: 11 & Prov. 15: 3 & Eph. 1: 23)
    m. (Gen. 18: 18 & Psa. 139: 1-16 & I Pet. 1: 2 & I Jn. 3: 20)

2. (Acts 2: 4); (Jn. 4: 23)

3. (Jn. 20: 31)

4. John:

    a. (John 1)
    b. (John 3)
    c. (John 4)
    d. (John 6)
    e. (John 8)
    f. (John 9)
    g. (John 10)
    h. (John 11)
    i. (John 12)
    j. (John 14)
    k. (John 15)
    l. (John 19)
    m. (John 19); (John 22)

5. (Phil. 3: 3)

6. (I Pet. 2: 5)

7. (Rev. 15: 4)

end of Topic # 5

Notes:

Topic # 6

Hope/Faith—Section # 1

Hope:

What is hope?

1. "Now, Lord, what wait I for? My hope (   ) is in thee." You might ask, what exactly do you mean by hope? Hope is to wish for something with expectation of its fulfillment and fulfill means to satisfy (c). Better stated, Biblical hope is imagining what it is in God's Word that we are desiring. We are instructed in (   ) to cast down those imaginations that exalt themselves against the knowledge of God, His Word. There are vain imaginations and good imaginations which are our hope.

2. Now think again and determine if your hopes line up with the Word of God. "Blessed is the man that trusteth in the Lord, (   ) and whose hope the Lord is."

3. Have you searched the scriptures regarding your hopes? Patience and comfort of the scriptures feeds (   ) our hope.

4. Even when there's endurance involved, we still have a God of hope that wants to fill us with joy and peace in believing (   ) through the power of the Holy Ghost within us.

5. Abraham certainly endured who against hope believed (   ) in hope.

6. When we hope (   ) for what we see not; we wait with patience.

7. Are you ready to give an answer for the hope (   ) that is within you? If your hopes don't line up with the Word of God, some changes need to be made in your desires.

8. Let's assume Jesus Christ is your Lord, you have checked out the Word of God, and your hopes do line up. Now we can continue. (   ) tells us the hope of the righteous shall be gladness.

Next you'll find some of the blessings we can hope for:

9. Carefully read chapter one of Ephesians. This letter was written to believers. Now fill in the blanks:

    a. We are blessed with all spiritual blessings (   ).

    b. God has abounded toward us in all wisdom (   ).

c. We are sealed with the Holy Spirit (   ).

d. We can know what is the hope of His calling, and
    what is the riches of the glory of His inheritance in us
    (   ).

e. We can understand what is the exceeding greatness of His
    power to us who believe (   ). And (Mt.   )
    tells us that all power was given back to Jesus and He gave
    us the authority to use His name.

f. Christ is our head and all things are under His feet
    (   ).

g. g & h are not from Eph. Greater is He who is within
    (I Jn.   ) you.

h. Search the scriptures for what you need and believe God
    will supply. What things soever you desire when you pray,
    believe (Mk.   ).

10. Are you looking for that blessed hope, (   ) the
    glorious appearing of the great God and our Saviour Jesus
    Christ?

11. The same Spirit (power) that raised Jesus from the dead (   ) dwells in you! That's the Spirit of Father God, God Almighty! He dwells in me/you! We're redeemed! He loves us!

12. Faith is the substance of things (   ) hoped for.

Let's move on into faith.

Topic # 6   Answer Sheet, Hope

1. (Psa. 39: 7); (II Cor. 10: 4-5)

2. (Jere. 17: 1)

3. (Rom. 15: 4)

4. (Rom. 15: 13)

5. (Rom. 4: 18)

6. (Rom. 8: 25)

7. (I Pet. 3: 15)

8. (Prov. 10: 28)

9. Blessings:

    a. (Eph. 1: 3)
    b. (Eph. 1: 8)
    c. (Eph. 1: 13)
    d. (Eph. 1: 18)
    e. (Eph. 1: 19); (Mt. 28: 18-20)
    f. (Eph. 1: 22)

       g.   (I Jn. 4: 4)
       h.   (Mk. 11: 24)

10. (Titus 2: 13)

11. (Rom. 8: 11)

12. (Heb. 11: 1)

end of Topic # 6

Notes:

Topic # 7

Hope/Faith—Section # 2

Faith:

1. We're ready to look at faith. The dictionary meaning is belief that does not rest on logical proof or material evidence; a secure belief. Secure means reliable, dependable; free from fear, anxiety or doubt. Sounds like scripture, doesn't it? "God has not given us the spirit (   ) of fear" and "Now, faith (   ) is the substance of things hoped for, the evidence of things not seen." Substance is everything one needs to build or complete something. Thus, all the ingredients or materials your need requires are there in your faith. God's power will do the assembling/building.

2. God has given to everyone the measure of faith (   ).

3. If the Word of God says it, faith can obtain it. Without faith (   ) it's impossible to please God. We are to believe He is God and that He is a rewarder of them that diligently seek him. Remember at the beginning, we were to search the Word of God!

4. Abraham believed God (   ) and called those things which be not as though they were and he became the father of many nations.

5. Whatever you ask in prayer, believe and you shall receive (&   &   ).

6. The trial of our faith is to result (   ) in praise, honor and glory.

We're working toward lining up our desires/attitudes (topic #2) with God's desires in order to walk in victory.

It all starts with thoughts (Topic #1). So, study the Word (Topic #1) and spend time with God. Hope (Topic #6) will become faith (Topic #7) as we study meditate, and speak God's Word.

Our mouth releases words (Topic 3) of faith and God's creative power does the work. We are to fight the good fight of faith (Topic # 7) by resisting attacks of sickness (Topic # 8) and afflictions (Topic # 9) with (Topic # 11) spiritual warfare and prayer (Topic # 10). Thank God for His grace and His Word.

7. We can develop our faith to appropriate God's promises. The Word of God instructs us to do the following:

a. Above all take (   ) the shield of faith to quench
    all the fiery darts of the wicked; see Topic # 11.

b. Spend much time daily with God; abide in Him
    (   ).

c. Faith comes by hearing the Word (   ) of God so

d. study & meditate on the Word (   ) and

e. renew your mind (   ).

f. Memorize the Word, it's able to make you wise unto
    salvation and is inspired of God to help you mature
    (   ).

g. Believe the Word & speak the Word (   ). Faith
    comes by hearing the Word (   ).

h. It's possible to have faith and unbelief at the same time.
    The writer of Hebrews tells us of the Israelites who
    saw and were a part of many miracles but did not enter
    (   ) because of their unbelief.

i. Unbelief can prevent the answer you're believing for from
    coming to pass. This scripture (   ) tells us that
    prayer and fasting can help remove the unbelief. There's

never (   ) anything lacking in the name of Jesus; speak words of faith to release the power—have faith (   ) and doubt not.

j.   Unbelief can come from the cares of this world, like daily living and what other people say, (   ) choking the Word.

k.   Praying in the spirit builds us up (&   ).

l.   The thief comes . . . but Jesus came that we might have life and have it more (   ) abundantly.

Faith cannot be linked to our goodness. If we believe we have to be or do something instead of believing in God's power and goodness alone, we have defiled our faith. God provides the grace and our faith is a positive response to what God has already promised. Faith appropriates what God has already provided by grace. Remember Gal. 5: 6 tells us that faith works by love and Jesus said in Mt. 22: 37-40 the great commandment is love.

Below are some promises in God's Word to consider:

Psa. 84: 11: *For the Lord God is a sun and shield: the Lord will give grace and glory: no good thing will he withhold from them that walk uprightly.*

Psa. 103: 2-5: *Bless the Lord, O my soul, and forget not all his benefits: Who forgiveth all thine iniquities; who healeth all they diseases.*

Mt. 7: 7-8: *Ask, and it shall be given you; seek, and ye shall find; knock, and it shall be opened unto you: For every one that asketh receiveth; and he that seeketh findeth; and to him that knocketh it shall be opened.*

Jas. 1: 5: *If any of you lack wisdom, let him ask of God, that giveth to all men liberally . . . .*

Heb. 13: 6: *So that we may boldly say, The Lord is my helper, and I will not fear what man shall do unto me.*

I Pet. 2: 24: *Who his own self bare our sins in His own body on the tree, that we, being dead to sins, should live unto righteousness: by whose stripes ye were healed.*

That last scripture leads us right into the next topic—Healing.

Topic # 7   Answer Sheet, Faith

1. (II Tim. 1: 7); (Heb. 11: 1)

2. Rom. 12: 3)

3. (Heb. 11: 6)

4. (Rom. 4: 17-18)

5. (Mt. 21: 21-22 & Mk. 11: 24 & I Jn. 5: 14-15)

6. (I Pet. 1: 7)

7. a. (Eph. 6: 16)
   b. (Jn. 15: 4)
   c. (Rom. 10: 17)
   d. (II Tim. 2: 15)
   e. (Rom. 12: 2)
   f. (II Tim. 2: 15-16)
   g. (Mk. 11: 23-24); (Rom. 10: 17)
   h. (Heb. 4: 18-19)
   i. (Mt. 17: 20); (Mt. 28: 18); (Mt. 21: 21)

j.   (Mk. 4: 19)

k.   (Jude 1: 20 & I Cor. 14: 18)

l.   (Jn. 10: 10)

end of Topic # 7

Notes:

Topic # 8

Healing

There's spiritual good sense to the order of these lessons. Our spiritual growth begins with knowing Jesus. We make a decision to receive Jesus and our relationship with Him grows by studying the Word. That same Word teaches us what to think and speak regarding healing.

It's important that proper speaking accompany believing for healing and of course we think thoughts before we speak. Faith is required for healing and hope comes into us before faith.

Let's begin to line up our thinking and speaking about divine healing with the Word of God.

1. Did Jesus pay for healing as well as our salvation at the same event? Is it God's will for believers in Jesus to be healed? What does God's Word declare? By Jesus' stripes we <u>were</u> healed (   ). That sounds like the work has already been completed.

2. It's just like our salvation. The price has been paid. He paid for all, not some, of our diseases (   ). Jesus never mentioned partial healing, delayed healing, or any particular ailment that will not get healed.

3. Perhaps if we spend some time searching out the price Jesus actually paid for our healing, it may become more real to us. Redemption means deliverance upon payment of ransom; to set free *(c)*. Are you a child of God? Have you received Jesus as your Lord and Saviour? Could anyone talk you out of that or are you totally and completely convinced that you are saved? The blood was shed on the cross to pay for our sins. Without the shedding of blood (   ) there is no remission. What was all that other torture about/for?

4. Let's first look in the Gospel of Matthew at the price paid. A great multitude with swords and staves (   ) came after Jesus and look—the chief priests and elders were there!

5. They spit in his face (   ), struck Him with their fists; and slapped Him in the face! This was also prophesied in (   ).

6. More of what was done to Jesus before the cruel crucifixion is found in the next chapter. He was flogged (to beat severely with a whip or rod *(c)*), crowned with thorns, mocked, spit upon, (NIV   &   ) and struck on the head again and again!

7. Pilate took Jesus, and scourged (   ) Him. Scourge used as a noun is a whip used to inflict punishment. As a verb

to scourge is a means of inflicting severe suffering, vengeance, punishment or to afflict with severe or widespread suffering and devastation; ravage, to chastise severely or to flog *(c)*!

8. Jesus and His Word are one (   ). If he said by His stripes we were healed, then we were healed. The price has been paid.

Why did Jesus subject Himself to all that? The song "Oh how He loves us" comes to my mind. His love is documented throughout the Word of God.

9. The Word of God states He heals all (   ) our diseases. We know it's not that easy sometimes if there are symptoms in our body or if we just received a bad report. So what's the answer? If the work has been done, then our receivers need repaired.

10. Jesus healed all (   ) who came to Him <u>believing</u>.

11. Jesus also said greater works (   ) than these <u>shall you do</u>.

12. After His resurrection the Word states all power (&   ) is given unto me (Jesus); go ye therefore; I am with you always.

13. The same spirit that raised Jesus (   ) from the dead dwells in believers. After the ascension, Jesus' disciples utilized that power to heal:

    a. In the name of Jesus Christ of Nazareth rise
        (&   ) up and walk.

    b. (NIV   ) Many paralytics and cripples were healed. You might ask why does it say many. I don't know (see # 10) but I know it does not say the power was not available to heal those who did not get healed. That's where we're going with this lesson.

    c. Peter raised Tabitha from the dead (   ) by the power available to him as a believer in Jesus.

    d. Paul perceived the crippled <u>man</u> (   ) <u>had</u> <u>faith to be healed</u> and he was healed.

    e. Eutychus was raised (   ) from death.

There are many more healings and miracles recorded in the book of Acts but now we will check out some scriptures on how to receive:

14. How did we get saved? Believe on the Lord Jesus Christ; so #1—believe. Back to the dictionary: believe—To have faith,

confidence or trust and to expect. Thus, believing for healing means to expect the healing to take place. Believe that those things which he says (   ) shall come to pass; he shall have whatsoever he says.

15. How are your expectors? The next verse (   ) states, whatever things you desire believe that you receive them, and you shall have them. All we need is faith the size of (   ) a mustard seed.

16. After believing for salvation, we (   ) spoke with our mouth to make it real. With the mouth confession is made unto salvation. Thus, for healing, believe and confess that healing when you speak.

17. Circumstances and people around us may want to get us to confess otherwise but the Word of God is still true—Jesus' stripes paid for that healing. If we allow the cares of this world (   ) . . . and other things to choke the Word, it becomes unfruitful.

18. It's hard work to resist everything (   ) that's screaming at us and seek ye first the kingdom of God. However; Thy Word (   ) is truth.

19. I'll close with this; speak to that mountain (   ) and receive your healing! *Please turn to the Appendix to Healing.*

Appendix to Healing

There were no such things as flavor enhancers, artificial colors and sweeteners, other additives, chemical ingredients, processed or fast food when the Bible was written. Therefore, they are not directly addressed in the Bible. Adam and Eve ate only fruits and vegetables (Gen. 1: 29) but that was before the flood.

Knowing the body is being properly nourished and exercised can negate some unbelief when one is believing God for healing. Thus, it's easier to reach out in faith for divine health. It is recommended that study be pursued regarding nutrition and health as it relates to our food supply today.

The Word of God teaches in I Corinthians 3: 16-17 that our bodies are the temple of the Holy Ghost so eating properly is good stewardship of our temples. The scripture we need here is James 1: 5-8; ask God for wisdom on this subject and He will give it to you.

We just learned to <u>believe that we receive</u>, and we will have it!
Don't forget about forgiveness (Topic #2).
Healing is a blessing; now let's move into joy and peace.

Topic # 8   **Answer Sheet, Healing**

1. (I Pet. 2: 24)

2. (Psa. 103: 2-3)

3. (Heb. 9: 22)

4. (Mt. 26: 47-50)

5. (Mt. 26: 67); (Isa. 50: 6)

6. (NIV Mt. 27: 28-30 & Mk. 15: 17-20)

7. (Jn. 19: 1)

8. (Jn. 1: 1)

9. (Psa. 103: 2-3)

10. (Lk. 6: 19)

11. (Jn. 14: 12)

12. (Mt. 28: 18 & Mk. 16: 18)

13. (Rom 8: 11)

a)   (Acts 3: 6 & 4: 10)
b)   (NIV Acts 8: 7)
c)   (Acts. 9: 40)
d)   (Acts. 14: 8-10)
e)   (Acts 20: 10)

14. (Mk. 11: 23)

15. (Mk. 11: 24); (Lk. 17: 6)

16. (Rom. 10: 10)

17. (Mk. 4: 19)

18. (Mt. 6: 31-34); (Jn. 17: 17)

19. (Mk. 11: 23)

end of Topic # 8

Notes:

Topic # 9

Peace/Joy

What is peace?—<u>Freedom from quarrels and disagreement</u>; harmonious relations; inner contentment; free from strife (c). Below we define a couple words that appear to be the opposite of peace:

strife:—<u>struggle, fight or quarrel; conflict, contention</u> (c).

stress:—A mentally or emotionally disruptive or upsetting condition occurring in <u>response to adverse external influences</u> characterized by increased heart rate, a rise in blood pressure, muscular tension, irritability, and depression (c).

God's Word always gives the answers:

1. Abram said unto Lot, (   ) Let there be no strife, between me and thee, for we be brethren.

2. Strive not with a man (   ) without cause.

3. If thy brother shall trespass against thee, (   ) go and tell him his fault between thee and him alone.

4. Do nothing out of selfish ambition (NIV   ) or vain conceit.
   Your attitude should be the same (NIV   ) as that of
   Christ Jesus.

5. He that is of a proud heart (   ) stirs up strife.

6. If it be possible, as much as lies in you, (   ) live
   peaceably with all men.

7. A wrathful man (   ) and hatred (   ) stirs
   up strife; but love covers all sins.

8. It looks like we're back to Topic # 2, Attitude, walking in love
   and forgiveness. The more excellent way (   ). We
   could all use less stress in our lives; trust God and pursue
   peace—inner contentment.

Dictionary time: joy,—A source or an object of pleasure or
satisfaction; to enjoy; to rejoice.

What should our source or object of pleasure be? We know the
answer to that. It's not the wrong kinds of pleasures such as the
following:

9. Those choked with cares and riches and (   )
   pleasures of this world do not have joy.

10. Unbelievers can be enslaved by serving divers lusts
(   ) and pleasures.

11. Folly is joy to him that is (   ) destitute of wisdom.

That more excellent way from (I Cor. 13) is demonstrated in (NIV Jas. 1: 2). If we walk in love, even when we face trials joy can be present. And affliction is mentioned in (I Thess. 1: 6) with joy of the Holy Ghost. Jesus desires that His joy might remain in us (Jn. 15:11) and our joy be full because the joy of the Lord (Neh. 8: 10) is our strength.

12. Jesus loves us so much He wants to bless us! Ask,
(   ) and ye shall receive, that your joy may be full.

13. John wrote his first letter to believers declaring what he had seen and heard of the Lord Jesus Christ (   ) that our joy might be full.

14. Our source of joy, as believers (&   ) in the Lord Jesus Christ is our God and what He has done for us.

15. Rejoice because your names are written (   ) in heaven.

16. (&   ) tells us to make a joyful noise unto the Lord.

The following verses refer to both peace and joy:

Rejoice in the Lord always . . . be anxious for nothing . . . and the peace of God which passes all understanding (   ) will keep your hearts and minds through Jesus Christ! We have righteousness, (   ) peace, and joy in the Holy Ghost and the fruit of the spirit (   ).

Now we should be ready to pray.

Topic # 9   Answer Sheet, Peace/Joy

1. (Gen. 13: 8)

2. (Prov. 3: 30)

3. (Matt. 18: 15)

4. (NIV Phil. 2: 3); (NIV Phil. 2: 5)

5. (Prov. 28: 25)

6. (Rom. 12: 18)

7. (Prov. 15: 18); (Prov. 10: 12)

8. (I Cor. 13)

9. (Lk. 8: 14)

10. (Titus 3: 3)

11. (Prov. 15: 21)

12. (Jn. 16: 24)

13. (I Jn. 1: 4)

14. (Jn. 17: 20-23 & Mt. 28: 18-20)

15. (Lk. 10: 20)

16. (Psa. 66: 1 & 81: 1)

17. (Phil. 4: 4-8); (Rom. 14: 17); (Gal. 5: 22)

end of Topic # 9

Notes:

Topic # 10

Prayer

1. **<u>What is prayer?</u>**

    a. Prayer can be both <u>worshipping</u> (&   )
        and <u>asking</u>.

    b. The people praying in the following scriptures were
        a (   ) certain ruler, a Canaanite woman
        (   ), and the mother of two of (   )
        Jesus' disciples. They all worshipped Jesus then made
        their request.

    c. Prayer can also be <u>thanking</u>
        (&   &   &   ).

    d. <u>Intercession</u> is mentioned throughout the New Testament.
        Paul said in (   ) I bow my knees unto the Father
        of our Lord Jesus Christ as he continued his prayer. The
        Spirit prays for us (   ).

2. **<u>Are there any pre-requisites to prayer?</u>**

    e. Here again we make a <u>choice.</u> Am I going to pray? The first
        step is to examine our own life, Topic # 2, (   ).

f. Is there any <u>unforgiveness</u> in me (   ); is there <u>unconfessed sin</u>? Judging others is addressed in (   ).

g. Are all my <u>attitudes</u> lined up with the Word of God? Do I love and/or care (&   &   ) about people and issues enough to <u>pray in faith</u> for change (   )?

3. **<u>Who</u> should pray and <u>where</u> should prayer take place?**

h. <u>Jesus</u> prayed (   ) and said prayer should be (   ) made <u>in secret</u>.

i. <u>Paul and Timothy</u> prayed <u>together</u> (   ) giving thanks to the Father for the believers and that they might be filled with the knowledge of God's will in all (   ) wisdom and spiritual understanding.

j. Believers <u>gathered together</u> (   ) <u>in a house</u> to pray in agreement.

k. <u>A widow</u> which departed not from the <u>temple</u> (   ) prayed <u>night and day</u>.

4. **<u>To whom</u> should we pray?**

77

l.   We are to pray to <u>Our Father</u> (   ) who is in Heaven.

m.   We are to ask the <u>Father</u> (   ) <u>in Jesus' name</u>. For there is one God and one mediator (   ) between God and man.

5. <u>How often should we pray?</u>

n.   We are to be <u>instant</u> (   ), which means to <u>continue and persevere,</u> in prayer. The NIV uses the word faithful.

o.   Pray <u>without ceasing</u> and with thanks (   ).

p.   I called unto the Lord in <u>distress</u> (   ). We never know when distress may come. Jonah's distress (   ) came from inside the belly of a great fish.

q.   My voice shalt thou hear in the morning, O Lord, (   ) in the <u>morning</u> will I direct my prayer unto thee.

6. <u>How do we pray?</u>

r.   The Lord taught His disciples to pray (&   ):

s.   Begin with praising Our Father in heaven;

t. glorifying His holy name and desiring His kingdom to come.

u. Ask that His will be done here in our situations.

v. Request with expectation that our daily need be filled, and

w. that He will forgive us our sins as we forgive. If we do not forgive, He can not forgive.

x. Request that the Lord lead us away from temptation and evil.

y. This same scripture says "when you fast" so that is also an expected part of prayer at times. Keep in mind that this passage was not meant to be a prayer/ritual (   ) just to be repeated.

z. <u>Ask, seek, knock</u>, (&   )

aa. Pray <u>in faith</u> (&   &   ) and <u>speak to the need</u> (   ).

bb. Make your requests in (   ) <u>prayer and supplication with thanksgiving</u>.

cc. Peter <u>knelt</u> down and prayed (   ) and raised Tabitha from the dead.

7. Who/what should we pray for:

dd. First we are to pray for (   ) <u>those in authority</u> over us.

ee. Love your enemies and pray for them who (   ) <u>despitefully use you and persecute you.</u>

ff. If you abide in Jesus, your desires will line up with His will and you can ask <u>whatever you will</u> (   ) and it will be done.

gg. We may ask <u>anything</u> in the name of Jesus that <u>glorifies the Father</u> and it (&   ) will be granted.

8. What does prayer produce?

hh. Prayer will produce <u>whatever you ask</u> if you follow God's directions. Some of these scriptures (&   ) above could result in your joy being full.

ii. A result of prayer in (   ) was the place was shaken where they were assembled together and they were all <u>filled with the Holy Ghost.</u>

jj. In the day when I cried (   ) thou answered
me, and strengthened me with strength in my soul.

kk. An important scripture regarding prayer for our nation is
(   ) *If my people, which are called by my name,
shall humble themselves, and pray, and seek my face, and
turn from their wicked ways; then will I hear from heaven,
and will forgive their sin, and will heal their land.*

ll. And we might close this section with the wonderful
amazing scripture that tells us our loving powerful God and
Father can do exceeding abundantly above all that we ask
or think, (   ) according to the power that works
in us.

Topic # 10   **Answer Sheet, Prayer**

a.   (Lk. 11: 9 & Mt. 7: 7)

b.   (Mt. 9: 18); (Mt. 15: 25-28); (Mt. 20: 20)

c.   (Phil. 1: 3 & Col. 1: 3 & II Thess. 1: 11 & Eph. 1: 15-19)

d.   (Eph. 3: 14-19): (Rom. 8: 26)

e.   (Mt. 7: 20-23)

f.   (Mk. 11: 25-26); (Mt. 7: 1-5)

g.   (Mk. 12: 31 & Jn. 13: 34-35 & Jn. 15: 12); (Mk. 11: 23-24)

h.   (Mk. 14: 32); (Mt. 6: 6)

i.   (Col. 1: 3); (Col. 1: 9-15)

j.   (Acts 12: 12)

k.   (Lk. 2: 37)

l.   (Mt. 6: 9)

m.   (Jn. 16: 23); (I Tim. 2: 5)

n.   (Rom. 12: 12)

o.   (I Thess. 5: 17-18)

p.   (Psa. 118: 5); (Jonah 2: 1)

q.   (Psa. 5: 3)

r.   r through x—(Mt. 6: 9-15 & Lk. 11: 2-4)

y.   (Mt. 6: 7)

z.   (Lk. 11: 9-10 & Mt. 7: 7-8)

aa. (Mt. 21: 21-22 & Lk. 17: 6 & Jas. 1: 6-8); (Mk. 11: 23)

bb. (Phil. 4: 6)

cc. (Acts 9: 40-41)

dd. (I Tim. 2: 1-5)

ee. (Mt. 5: 44)

ff.   (Jn. 15: 7)

gg. (Jn. 14: 13-14 & 16: 23-24)

hh. (Jn. 14: 14 & Jn. 16: 24)

ii.   (Acts 4: 31)

jj.   (Psa. 138: 3)

kk. (I Chr. 16: 11)

ll.   (Eph. 3: 20)

end of Topic 10

Notes:

Topic # 11

Spiritual Warfare

Before we begin, know that Satan's power has been taken from him. The only power he has in a Christian's life is what that person allows.

- (Col 2:15) He (Jesus) had disarmed the rulers and authorities of darkness. He made a public display of them, having triumphed over them.

- (Mat. 28: 18) After Jesus' resurrection He told His disciples that "All authority has been given to Me in heaven and on earth." He commissioned us to have authority by using His name. Then in verse 20 He promised "I am with you always, even to the end of the age".

Look at how we get anything in the spiritual realm. For example, salvation is received by believing in your heart and confessing with your mouth the Lord Jesus and you shall be saved (Rom. 10: 9-10). No one can be saved without first knowing/learning about the Savior. We know spiritual truths by reading and studying the Word of God. Believe—speak—receive.

The Word tells us in Jas. 4: 7 to submit to God, resist the devil and he will flee from you. That word resist means to strive to fend off or offer actions; to remain firm against; to keep from giving in or enjoying; to offer resistance (c).

The devil prowls around <u>as</u> a roaring lion (I Pet. 5: 6-8) and he has no power unless we submit to his lies, believe them, and speak them. Greater is He that is in you, than he that is in the world (I Jn. 4: 4).

Satan can not do anything against us unless we enable him. II Cor. 10: 4-5 tells us to cast down every imagination that exalts itself against the knowledge of God and bring into captivity every thought to the obedience of Christ. We are instructed in Phil. 4: 8 what we are allowed to think about and it must be a good report.

What does God's Word say about your situation? Phil. 4: 13 "I can do all things through Christ which strengthens me." Phil. 4:19 "My needs are met according to God's riches in glory by Christ Jesus." I Pet. 2:24 "By Jesus' stripes, I was healed." Isa. 54: 17 "No weapon formed against me shall prosper." Gal. 3: 29 "I am Abraham's seed and heir according to the promise."

Add your own scripture promises that pertain to your life. Jn. 17:17 "Thy Word is truth", believe it.

Now you are ready to look at Eph. 6: 10-18.

The armor of God is not a "once a day" activity; it is a way of life. In order for it to work, we must be saved. Salvation and righteousness go together; we are saved through the blood of Jesus and the Holy Spirit is in our spirit giving us righteousness, peace and Joy. The sword of the spirit is the Word of God and we are to speak the Word of God not our circumstances, feelings, or problems. Speak the Word that is applicable and those feelings/emotions will come into line with truth (Jas. 3). The Word of God is truth! God has given to every born again believer the measure of faith (Rom. 12:3) and our faith matures (Rom. 10:17) as we read, study, meditate and speak the Word of God. That faith quenches all the fiery darts of the enemy (Eph. 6: 16).

We release our faith by speaking the Word that pertains to our life:

- I am saved through the blood of Jesus. See Page # 3 at the beginning of this workbook and also Jn. 14: 6; (helmet) I am the righteousness of God (breastplate) and the Holy Spirit is in me. (Rom. 14: 17) I have peace and joy.
- No weapon that is formed against me shall prosper . . . (Isa. 54: 17).
- (Jas. 4: 7) I submit myself to God, I resist the devil, and he has to flee from me. The Word of God declares that greater is He who is in me than he who is in the world (I Jn. 4: 4) and God's Word is truth (belt of truth).
- You have the authority to speak to the enemy in the name of Jesus: I take authority over the devil and every evil spirit that would try to come against me; (Mt. 18: 18) they are bound and powerless in my life. My needs are met according to God's riches in glory by Christ Jesus (Phil. 4: 19).

- I am strong in the Lord and the power of His might (Eph. 6: 10).
- And lastly don't forget to live in praise. (I Thess. 5: 18) Praise God in everything and (Heb. 12: 2) fix your eyes on Jesus the author and finisher of your faith.

So again we come back to the truth that without daily reading, studying, meditating and speaking the Word our victory will not be complete.

When we fill ourselves with God's Word, we will share the Gospel with others at every opportunity (Gospel of peace) and in order to pray in the Holy Spirit we must be baptized in the Holy Ghost (Acts 1: 5 & 2: 4). Praying in the spirit is not only the rest and refreshing prophesied in Isa. 28: 11-12 also, the Holy Spirit prays the prayers that need prayed when we don't know how to pray (Rom. 8: 26).

Every part of the armor involves the Word of God. Study the Word daily and develop your faith in God (Rom. 10: 17) and in His Word.

Fill yourself with the Word of God as much as your day will allow— make time. Draw nigh to God, (Jas. 4: 8) and he will draw nigh to you.

Fill your day with praise and thanksgiving; focus on God and His goodness. The armor of God protects us as we practice these truths and incorporate them into our lives.

Enjoy your Victory!

Notes:

Conclusion

We began by attempting to decide what we should focus on for total victory in our lives. Let's take a look at life in general.

Life—daily living—what do we deal with? Oh, it's a combination of many issues both good and some not so good. For example, daily responsibilities, we all have them. How do we respond? We have a choice.

There are people who are sometimes a blessing and sometimes they are difficult. We could be offended and even spoken wrongfully about. Sometimes abuses occur and troubles result from other people's wrong choices. That leads to our attitude and we always have a choice.

Health is always part of our lives. Attacks of sickness and disease are common to the human race. Good health is a blessing. What do we do when sickness attacks us and/or our family? Looks like another choice!

How about finances? Do we always have what we think we need and do we have what we want? Is there enough work or is there too much? What can we do to better our situation? Is this another choice to make?

On and on—neighbors, transportation, national economy, world conditions all fill our days. Even weather conditions can affect our decisions. We're constantly bombarded with choices and we may not even be aware of it. That's called life. Do we just react naturally or do we take time to reflect on what God would have us do? The world reacts naturally; we have the option to consult the Lord and His Holy Word. The more of it we memorize and understand the better and less difficult our choices will be. God's choices will lead to a more joyful productive life.

We started trying to find the common thought throughout all the studies. If you go back and look, you will find that knowing the Word of God is paramount in each topic. Fill your mind and heart with it; Psalm 119: 97-105 tells us the Word makes wise, gives understanding, good judgment and is a lamp to our feet! Wow!

The Lord bless thee, and keep thee: The Lord make his face shine upon thee, and be gracious unto thee: The Lord lift up his countenance upon thee, and give thee peace. (Numbers 6: 24-26)